Welcome to this book!
Are you a coffee lover?
Do you enjoy the aroma and taste of coffee?
Do you like experimenting
with different ingredients?
Have you ever thought of cooking with coffee?
What if there is more to using coffee instead
of just drinking it?
If you have entertained these thoughts,
this is the perfect book for you!

© Copyright 2021
All rights reserved: Ivan Nossa, **Cuore d'oro libri**
www.cuoredorolibri.com
info@ivannossa.com
The content contained within this book may not be reproduced, duplicated or transmitted without direct written permission from the author or the publisher.

Under no circumstances will any blame or legal responsibility be held against the publisher, or author, for any damages, reparation, or monetary loss due to the information contained within this book, either directly or indirectly.

Legal Notice
This book is copyright protected. It is only for personal use. You cannot amend, distribute, sell, use, quote or paraphrase any part, or the content within this book, without the consent of the author or publisher.

Disclaimer Notice
Please note the information contained within this document is for educational and entertainment purposes only. All effort has been executed to present accurate, up to date, reliable, complete information. No warranties of any kind are declared or implied. Readers acknowledge that the author is not engaged in the rendering of legal, financial, medical or professional advice. The content within this book has been derived from various sources. Please consult a licensed professional before attempting any techniques outlined in this book.

By reading this document, the reader agrees that under no circumstances is the author responsible for any losses, direct or indirect, that are incurred as a result of the use of the information contained within this document, including, but not limited to, errors, omissions, or inaccuracies.

VV.AA.

Cooking With Coffee

*Ideas and Recipes
for Coffee Lovers*

Table of Contents

7 **Introduction**

9 **Chapter 1**
Learning More About Coffee
10 History of Coffee
11 How Is Coffee Made?
11 Types of Coffee Beans
13 Tips to Remember While Cooking With Coffee

15 **Chapter 2**
Coffee Based Appetizers
16 Maple Bacon Coffee Deviled Eggs
17 Chocolate Coffee "Graham" Crackers
19 Sweet Rhode Island Coffee-Dunked Turkey Appetizer Meatballs
21 Coffee Flavored Cheesy Potato Cups
23 Sweet & Spicy Jerky
25 Black Bean Dip
27 Coffee Flavored Fruit Dip
28 Coffee and Walnut Cake Balls
30 Espresso-Brined Chicken Drummettes
32 Coffee-Glazed Golden Beet Salad
34 Cocoa Cardamom Espresso Roasted Almonds

37 **Chapter 3**
Main Dish Recipes
38 Swedish Meatballs
41 Prime Rib Roast
43 Caramelized Coffee Spiced Chicken
45 Coffee-Brined Chicken Drumsticks
47 Coffee-Rubbed Pork Roast
48 Roasted Portobello Steaks With Walnut Coffee Sauce
50 Ham With Red-Eye Gravy
52 Salmon Tacos With Coffee Rub
55 Risotto with Capers and Espresso

57	**Chapter 4**
	Dessert Recipes
58	Coffee Ice Cream
60	Chocolate Coffee Toffee Crunch Muffins
63	Double Chocolate Bundt Cake with Ganache Glaze
66	Vietnamese Coffee Sundaes With Crushed Peanut Brittle
68	Chocolate Pudding
70	Bittersweet Chocolate Tart With Coffee Mascarpone Cream
73	Mini Tiramisu
77	**Chapter 5**
	Drink Recipes
78	Choco Fudge Protein Shake
80	The Layaway
81	Siciliano
82	Iced Coffee Shakerato
83	Iced Horchata Latte
85	Mochatini (Mocha Martini)
86	Caramel Irish Coffee
87	Coffee Smoothie
89	Mint Mojito Iced Coffee
90	Salted Caramel Mocha Coffee Concentrate
93	**Chapter 6**
	Uses of Coffee in Your Home
94	To Remove Odor From Your Refrigerator
94	To Remove Odor From Hands
95	As a Fertilizer
95	To Clean Dishes
96	To Clean Grill and Stains on Kitchen Tiles
96	To Clean and Repair Scratches on Wooden Furniture
96	To Clean Drains
97	To Repel Fleas From Pets
97	To Clean Countertops
98	**Conclusion**
101	**Suggested Readings**
103	**References**

Introduction

I want to thank you for choosing this book, *Cooking With Coffee: Ideas and Recipes for Coffee Lovers*.
Even if you start your daily routine with a cup of coffee, there is no rule that it needs to end there. Coffee has a unique flavor profile and aroma which instantly adds depth and richness to any recipe. Cooking with coffee will truly change how you view this humble ingredient.
In this book, you'll discover several recipes that you can easily make using coffee. Coffee can be easily incorporated into syrups, vinaigrette, spice rubs, meat dishes, baked goodies, desserts, and even drinks. All these recipes will introduce you to various delicious flavor combinations and pairings that will quickly elevate your cooking game. Cooking with coffee has never been this interesting or delicious.
The recipes given are simple, even for a novice cook. You don't need to spend hours in the kitchen. With these recipes, you can whip up gourmet dishes and drinks within no time! Before you start cooking, ensure that you have all the required ingredients including good quality coffee on hand.

Once these things are in place, you merely need to select a recipe that interests you, follow the simple instructions, and voila! Yes, it is as simple as that. So, are you excited to experiment with all these delicious recipes? If yes, then let's get started on this culinary experience without much further ado.

Chapter 1

Learning More About Coffee

The first thing we think of when it comes to coffee is the wafting aroma and steaming mugs filled with our daily dose of caffeine—or maybe Starbucks! We are all used to drinking coffee, but did you ever wonder where coffee came from or how humans started the consumption of coffee? Here is a quick look at everything you need to know about coffee.

History of Coffee

The unanimous opinion is that coffee originated somewhere in the Ethiopian highlands. One of the popular origin stories of coffee is that a goat herder in the 9th century noticed how active his goats were after consuming berries from a tree. This goat herder quickly contacted the local monastery to let them know about his observation. A monk was inspired to make a brew from the said berries. To his delight, he discovered that this brew helped him stay awake for longer than usual. Gradually the news of this brilliant discovery about the wonder brew spread to Egypt and the Arabian peninsula. This is how coffee started traveling across the globe (Oxenreider, 2013).

How Is Coffee Made?

So, how is coffee made? During spring, coffee trees usually blossom with pretty white flowers. These flowers turn into small green beans which further ripen into berries that look like cherries. These berries are later hand-picked by fall. The conventional method of making coffee involves sun-drying the berries until the moisture level reduces to 10%. This process usually takes several weeks, and it is still practiced in several countries across the globe. A modern method that's commonly used involves the removal of the berry pulp mechanically, after which the beans are dried. After this, the berries are mechanically hulled wherein the outer husk is removed. This process produces pure green beans that need to be roasted. These green beans are later washed and sorted according to their size. Once the coffee beans are roasted, they are ground to make a fine powder. This is how coffee is made.

Types of Coffee Beans

Depending on how the coffee beans are picked and roasted and their country of origin, their flavor and taste vary. There are several varieties of coffees available in the market these days. Coffee beans are usually divided into four primary categories: Arabica, Robusta, Liberica, and Excelsa.

The most common and heavily marketed coffee beans found in North America is Arabica. It has a delicate flavor, is sweeter tasting than others, and is less acidic.

Robusta coffee beans are usually popular in the regions of Europe, Africa, and the Middle East. These beans have a strong aroma and are known for their robust flavor. This coffee variant also has high levels of caffeine when compared to the other three beans.

Liberica coffee beans are quite delightful and a rare treat for coffee lovers. They are usually grown in specific climatic conditions. Their production is too scarce for large scale operations or to satisfy global demand. These beans are quite a pleasant surprise with a woody aroma and taste.

The fourth type of coffee beans is Excelsa. Technically, this belongs to the Liberica coffee bean family. It is primarily grown in Southeast Asia and accounts for only a small fraction of global coffee production. It has a tart and a fruity flavor which is the perfect combination of light and dark roast coffee. Its unique profile makes it quite popular with coffee aficionados.

The only thing you need to remember while purchasing coffee is to buy a coffee blend that appeals to your taste palette. If you find something you enjoy, stick with it. Arabica and Robusta are the most affordable and widely available options these days. Why don't you try experimenting with a couple of different blends until you find something you enjoy? If you already have such a blend, use it for the recipes given in this book.

Tips to Remember While Cooking With Coffee

While using coffee, always remember that it pairs incredibly well with desserts and baked goodies. Whether it is tiramisu, muffins, or a chocolate cake, the flavor combinations will truly blow your mind. Don't just restrict yourself to desserts while cooking with coffee. Why don't you try incorporating coffee into drinks such as an iced horchata latte, mocha martini, or even a delicious cup of caramel Irish coffee? Coffee can also be added to savory items such as maple bacon or potato cups, main dishes including meatballs, beef, and pork roasts, and savory sauces or marinades. All the information you need to cook these delicious recipes and more are given in this book.

Whenever you are cooking with coffee, always opt for espresso or real coffee instead of instant coffee blends. If you are in a pinch, instant coffee blends will help, but do try real coffee if you want to truly elevate the flavor profile of the dishes you cook. As a rule of thumb, if a recipe calls for coffee grounds, avoid using wet ones. The coffee grounds need to be completely dry before you add them to a recipe, especially when it comes to spice rubs. Never use old or stale coffee while cooking. As with any other food product, even coffee becomes stale quite quickly. If a recipe calls for brewed coffee, ensure that you use freshly brewed coffee and not the stale coffee that's lying around. As long as you keep these simple tips in mind, you can certainly obtain the best results while cooking with coffee. So, let's dive into the recipes.

Chapter 2

Coffee Based Appetizers

Maple Bacon Coffee Deviled Eggs

Serves: 12

Ingredients

- 6 hard-boiled eggs, peeled, halved lengthwise
- 1 ½ teaspoons finely ground coffee + extra to garnish
- ¼ cup bacon crumbles, divided
- ⅓ cup mayonnaise
- 1 ½ teaspoons maple sugar + extra to garnish
- Sea salt to garnish

Directions

1. Carefully separate the yolks from the eggs and place them in a bowl.
2. Stir in mayonnaise, maple sugar, ground coffee, and half the bacon crumbles. You can also process it in a blender or food processor if you want it really smooth.
3. Transfer the contents in a piping bag and pipe it in the egg white cavities.
4. Garnish with coffee, sea salt, and maple sugar and serve.

Chocolate Coffee "Graham" Crackers

Serves: 6

Ingredients

- ¼ cup all-purpose flour
- 1 cup whole-wheat flour
- ½ teaspoon baking soda
- ½ cup packed dark brown sugar
- ¼ teaspoon kosher salt
- 3 tablespoons honey
- 1 tablespoon vanilla extract
- 1 teaspoon instant espresso powder
- 2 ½ tablespoons milk
- 1 tablespoon unsweetened cocoa powder
- 3 ½ tablespoons cold unsalted butter, diced

Directions

1. Place all-purpose flour, whole-wheat flour, baking soda, sugar, and salt in the food processor bowl and process well.
2. Scatter butter over the flour mixture. Give short pulses until butter is small in size.
3. Combine honey, cocoa, milk, espresso powder, and vanilla in a bowl and add it into the food processor and process until you get a dough consistency.

Appetizers

4. Keep the dough wrapped in cling wrap and refrigerate for 2 hours.
5. Preheat the oven to 350° F. Place a rack in the center of the oven.
6. Dust some flour on your countertop and place the dough on it and roll it until it is 1/8 inch in thickness. Take a sharp knife and cut into rectangles of 4 x 2 inches.
7. Place the crackers on the baking sheet. Pierce holes on top of the crackers with a toothpick.
8. Place the baking sheet in the oven and bake for 15 – 18 minutes or until dry and brown.
9. Let it cool for a few minutes on the baking sheet. Place the crackers on a cooling rack to cool completely.
10. Transfer into an airtight container until use.

Sweet Rhode Island Coffee-Dunked Turkey Appetizer Meatballs

∽ Serves: 4-6 ∽

Ingredients

For sauce:
- Hot sauce of your choice to taste
- 1 tablespoon chopped chipotle pepper in adobo sauce
- 1 ½ teaspoons rice vinegar
- ½ cup coffee syrup

For meatballs:
- 10 ounces lean turkey
- ¼ cup plain nonfat Greek yogurt
- ¼ teaspoon chili powder
- Freshly ground pepper to taste
- ¼ cup plain dry breadcrumbs
- 1 small egg
- Salt to taste

Directions

1. To make sauce: Combine chipotle pepper, hot sauce, rice vinegar, and coffee syrup in a skillet.
2. To make meatballs: Combine turkey, yogurt, chili powder, pepper, breadcrumbs, egg, and salt in another bowl.

Appetizers

3. Make meatballs from the mixture and place them on a prepared baking sheet.
4. Prepare the oven by preheating it to 350° F. Place a rack in the center of the oven.
5. Bake the meatballs in a preheated oven for about 20 – 25 minutes or until they turn brown and are cooked through. Turn the meatballs a couple of times while baking.
6. Transfer the meatballs into the sauce skillet. Stir the meatballs so that they are well coated with the sauce mixture.
7. Place the skillet over medium flame and heat thoroughly.
8. Transfer onto a serving platter. Insert toothpicks in each meatball and serve.

Coffee Flavored Cheesy Potato Cups

∽ Serves: 12 ∽

Ingredients

- 2 ½ tablespoons butter, melted, divided (use more if required)
- ¾ pound starchy potatoes like russet potatoes or Yukon gold potatoes or a mixture of both, peeled, cut into cubes of about 2 inches
- 1 ½ tablespoons strong coffee
- 3 ounces cheddar cheese, shredded + extra to top
- 2 tablespoons fine cracker crumbs or breadcrumbs
- 1 ½ tablespoons whole milk or half and half
- 1 ½ tablespoons sour cream
- ½ tablespoon minced chives or green onions
- Salt to taste
- Pepper to taste

Directions

1. Grease a 12-count muffin pan with a little of the melted butter. Sprinkle cracker crumbs on the bottom and sides of the cup.
2. Place potatoes in a pot. Pour enough cold water to cover the potatoes, about an inch above the potatoes. Place the pot over high flame. Cover the pot and let it come to a boil.

Appetizers

3. Lower the flame, uncover and cook until the potatoes are fork tender. Drain off the water and place the potatoes back in the pot. Let it heat for a few minutes until dry. Turn off the heat.
4. Combine milk, coffee, and remaining melted butter in a small saucepan. Heat the mixture until warm. Drizzle the mixture over the potatoes and mash using a potato masher.
5. Stir in sour cream, chives, and half the cheese. Place 2 teaspoons of the mashed potatoes in each of the muffin cups. Press it lightly onto the bottom of the cups.
6. Sprinkle remaining cheese into the cups. Place some more of the mashed potato mixture in the cups. Brush with some melted butter. Sprinkle some more cheese on top.
7. Preheat the oven to 350° F and place the muffin pan on the middle rack of the oven and bake for around 25 – 30 minutes.
8. Once ready, let them remain in the muffin pan for 5 – 6 minutes.
9. Run a knife around the edges of the potato cups and loosen the potato cups. Invert onto a wire rack and cool completely.
10. Serve.

Sweet & Spicy Jerky

∽ *Serves: 12* ∽

Ingredients

- ¾ cup brewed strong coffee
- 1 whole star anise pod
- ¼ cup Asian fish sauce
- 2 tablespoons sambal oelek
- ¾ cup Coca-Cola
- 1 cup soy sauce
- ¼ cup fresh lime juice
- 1 pound trimmed beef top round or bottom round, cut into ¼ inch thick slices

Appetizers

Directions

1. To make marinade: Pour coffee and Coca-Cola into a saucepan. Add star anise and place the saucepan over high flame. Let it cook until the liquid is half its original quantity. Turn off the heat.
2. Transfer the mixture into a bowl. Stir in fish sauce, soy sauce, sambal oelek, and lime juice.
3. Place beef in the marinade. Stir until beef is well combined with the marinade. Keep the bowl covered.
4. Place the bowl in the refrigerator for 6 – 8 hours.
5. Take out the meat pieces from the marinade and dry them by patting with paper towels.
6. Place meat pieces on the oven rack.
7. Bake in an oven that has been preheated to 200° F for around 4 hours and nearly dried fully, yet chewable. Cool to room temperature.
8. Store the jerky in an airtight container and refrigerate it. It should last for 5 – 6 weeks.

Black Bean Dip

Serves: 8 – 10

Ingredients

- 2 cans (30 ounces each) black beans, drained, rinsed
- 2 white onions, chopped
- 2 tablespoons minced garlic
- 2 teaspoons ground cumin
- 2 tablespoons sugar
- ½ cup brewed coffee or 1 tablespoon instant coffee mixed in ½ cup hot water
- 2 heaping teaspoons Better Than Bouillon
- 4 teaspoons dried Mexican oregano
- Hot sauce to taste
- 1 ½ cups unsalted butter
- 2 jalapeños, deseeded, chopped
- Salt to taste

Directions

1. Heat a large skillet over medium flame and add a dab of butter, then add onions and cook until it turns soft.
2. Stir in jalapeño, cumin, Better Than Bouillon, garlic, salt, and oregano and let it cook for a couple of minutes.

Appetizers

3 Add the beans and let it cook for 4 – 5 minutes.

4 Stir in sugar and hot sauce. Once sugar dissolves, turn off the heat.

5 Transfer the bean mixture into the food processor. Pour coffee and process until you get a smooth puree. Add more of the spices and salt if required.

6 Pour the dip into a bowl. Cover and set aside for 2 – 3 hours.

7 Serve with chips or vegetable sticks. It can also be used in burritos, wraps, quesadillas, etc.

Coffee Flavored Fruit Dip

Serves: 4 – 6

Ingredients

- 4 ounces cream cheese, softened
- ¼ cup brown sugar
- 4 ounces frozen whipped topping, thawed
- 4 ounces sour cream
- 3 tablespoons coffee-flavored liqueur

Directions

1. Combine sour cream, cream cheese, coffee-flavored liqueur, and brown sugar in a bowl.
2. Beat the mixture with an electric hand mixer for about 3 – 4 minutes.
3. Add whipped topping and fold gently.
4. Cover the bowl and chill until used. Serve with any fruit of your choice.

Appetizers

Coffee and Walnut Cake Balls

∽ *Serves: 6* ∽

Ingredients

- ½ cup pitted dates
- ½ cup walnuts
- ¼ teaspoon vanilla extract
- ¾ teaspoon instant coffee mixed with about 2 tablespoons boiling water

Directions

1. Transfer the walnuts in a food processor bowl and process until moist sand-like in texture.
2. Place dates and pulse until finely chopped and the mixture is well incorporated.
3. Pour vanilla and coffee into the processor bowl and pulse the mixture until well combined.
4. Make six equal portions and shape them into balls.
5. Keep the balls on a plate or tray and refrigerate it until further use. It can last for 10 days.

Espresso-Brined Chicken Drummettes

∽ *Serves: 6 – 8* ∽

Ingredients

- 1 pound chicken wings and drummettes, trimmed of excess fat, skin, and cartilage, rinsed
- ½ cup water
- 3 ½ teaspoons salt, divided
- ½ tablespoon ground pepper
- ¾ teaspoon garlic powder
- ¾ teaspoon dried oregano
- ¾ teaspoon dried thyme
- ¼ teaspoon cayenne pepper or to taste
- 1 teaspoon Spanish or sweet paprika
- ½ teaspoon poultry seasoning
- ½ cup strong brewed coffee or espresso, cooled
- 2 small bay leaves
- ½ tablespoon finely ground espresso beans
- 1 tablespoon pure maple syrup

Directions

1. Pour coffee and water into a bowl. Stir in bay leaves and 3 teaspoons salt and place the wings in it. Make sure wings are well covered in the brine.

2 Combine ½ teaspoon salt, spices, herbs and espresso beans in another bowl. Taste and adjust the seasonings if required.

3 Remove the chicken from the brine. Pat the chicken with paper towels until dry. Sprinkle the spice mixture all over the wings.

4 Place a rack on a baking sheet. Place the chicken on the rack.

5 Prepare the oven by preheating it to 350° F.

6 Place the rack along with the baking sheet in the oven and bake for 15 minutes.

7 Brush chicken lightly with maple syrup and continue baking for 10 minutes.

8 Set the oven to broil mode. Brush the chicken once again with maple syrup and broil for a few minutes (3 to 5 minutes).

Coffee-Glazed Golden Beet Salad

Serves: 3

Ingredients

For coffee glaze:
- ¼ cup brewed coffee
- 1 ½ tablespoons honey
- ½ teaspoon Dijon mustard
- 2 teaspoons balsamic vinegar
- ¼ teaspoon salt
- 2 tablespoons extra-virgin olive oil

For salad:
- 3 medium golden beets with greens
- 2 ounces feta cheese, crumbled
- Olive oil, as required

Directions

1. To make coffee glaze: Mix together coffee, honey, 1 ½ teaspoons vinegar, and salt in a saucepan.
2. Heat the saucepan over medium flame and let the mixture evaporate until it becomes half its actual quantity.
3. To make salad: Rinse the greens as well as beets and dry them as well. Tear the beet greens into pieces.

4. Place the beets with its peel on in a baking dish. Pour some oil over it and cover the baking dish. Place it in a preheated oven and bake at 375° F for 60 minutes or until tender.
5. Let them cool for a few minutes. Peel the beets now and chill for 30 – 40 minutes. Also chill the beet greens. Cut the beets into round slices.
6. To assemble: Place beet greens on the center of a serving platter. Place the beet slices around the beet greens. Sprinkle feta cheese on top.
7. Pour glaze on top and serve.

Appetizers

Cocoa Cardamom Espresso Roasted Almonds

∽ Serves: 18 – 20 ∽

Ingredients

- 1 cup granulated sugar
- 4 teaspoons instant espresso powder
- 1 teaspoon salt
- 2 tablespoons vanilla bean paste
- 4 tablespoons cocoa powder
- 3 teaspoons ground cardamom
- 2 egg whites
- 6 cups raw almonds

Directions

1. Prepare a large baking sheet by lining it with parchment paper. Prepare your oven by pre-heating it to 275° F.
2. Stir together cocoa powder, sugar, cardamom, espresso powder, and salt in a bowl until free from lumps.
3. Combine egg whites and vanilla bean paste in a bowl and whisk until some froth is formed.
4. Stir in the almonds. Add the cocoa powder mixture and stir until well combined.
5. Spread the almonds on the baking dish, in a single layer.
6. Place the baking dish in the oven and bake the almonds for about 25 minutes. Stir every 10 to 12 minutes.
7. Cool completely on the baking sheet making sure to stir often.
8. Transfer into an airtight container until use.

Chapter 3

Main Dish Recipes

Swedish Meatballs

Serves: 12

Main dish

Ingredients

- 3 cups soft bread crumbs
- 2 eggs, beaten
- ½ cup minced fresh parsley
- 2 teaspoons ground nutmeg
- 1 pound ground beef
- 1 pound ground veal
- 1 pound ground pork
- 2 cups half and half
- ⅔ cup chopped onion
- 2 teaspoons salt or to taste
- ½ teaspoon ground ginger

For gravy:
- 6 tablespoons all-purpose flour
- 1 cup hot brewed coffee
- 2 cans (14.5 ounces each) beef broth
- Hot cooked noodles to serve

Directions

1. Place bread crumbs in a bowl. Stir in the cream. Let it rest for 5 minutes.
2. Add eggs, parsley, nutmeg, onion, salt, and ginger. Mix well.
3. Add all the types of ground meat and mix until well combined.
4. Spray a baking sheet and baking dish with cooking spray.
5. Make 1 inch balls of the mixture and place on the baking sheet.
6. Prepare the oven by preheating it to 350° F.
7. Bake the meatballs in a preheated oven for about 20 – 25 minutes or until they become brown and are cooked through. Turn the meatballs a couple of times while baking.
8. Transfer the meatballs into the baking dish. Pour the cooked liquids into a saucepan.

Add flour and stir until well combined. Pour broth and coffee and whisk well.

9. Place the saucepan over medium flame. Stir constantly until thick. Pour the gravy over the meatballs. Stir the meatballs so that they are well coated with the gravy.

10. Place the baking dish in the oven and bake until heated thoroughly and the gravy is bubbling.

11. Serve over hot cooked noodles.

Main dish

Prime Rib Roast

Serves: 5

Ingredients

- 3 tablespoons finely ground coffee
- ½ tablespoon freshly ground pepper
- 1 6-pound bone-in prime rib roast
- Salt to taste
- ⅛ vanilla bean, split, seeds scraped

Directions

1. Combine coffee, pepper, salt, and vanilla bean seeds in a bowl.
2. Rub this mixture all over the rib roast and place it in a roasting pan, with the bone side down. Rub well on the fat part. Place it on your countertop for about 30 minutes.
3. Prepare the oven by preheating it to 450° F.
4. Place the roasting pan in the oven and roast for 15 minutes. Lower the oven temperature to 325° F and continue roasting for 15 minutes.
5. Place the roast on your cutting board and let it cool down for 20 minutes. Remove any extra rub by scraping it, if desired.

6 Cut into slices and serve with a side dish of your choice.

Main dish

Caramelized Coffee Spiced Chicken

Serves: 3 – 4

Ingredients

- 1 ½ tablespoons water
- 1 tablespoon orange juice
- 1 tablespoon seasoning of your choice
- 1 tbsp Black Dust Cowboy Coffee rub
- ½ tablespoon vegetable or olive oil
- 1 tablespoon brown sugar
- 1 tablespoon Baker's Brew Coffee Spice
- ¾ pound boneless, skinless chicken thighs
- 2 scallions, sliced
- 1 ½ tablespoons balsamic vinegar

Directions

1. Combine brown sugar, water, orange juice, seasonings, coffee rub, coffee spice, and vinegar in a bowl. Stir until brown sugar dissolves completely.
2. Place chicken in the bowl and turn the chicken around to coat well with the marinade. Chill for 1 – 4 hours.
3. Remove chicken from the bowl and retain the marinade. Dry the chicken by patting with paper towels.

Main dish

4 Heat a pan over medium flame. Heat some oil in the pan and place the chicken in the pan. Cook the chicken until it becomes brown from all sides. Once the chicken gets a desirable char, remove it from the pan and place in a bowl.

5 Pour the retained marinade into the pan. Lower the heat and cook until thick and glaze like.

6 Add chicken and scallions into the pan and stir well. Heat for a couple of minutes, stirring often.

7 Serve.

Coffee-Brined Chicken Drumsticks

Serves: 2

Ingredients

- ¾ cup brewed strong coffee
- 1 ½ tablespoons sugar
- ¼ teaspoon crushed red pepper
- 1 small stick cinnamon
- 2 tablespoons salt
- 1 tablespoon chili powder
- 2 cloves garlic, crushed
- 4 chicken drumsticks
- 1 cup water

Directions

1. Combine water, sugar, salt, and coffee in a bowl. Stir until the sugar dissolves completely.
2. Add spices and stir. Stir in the chicken. Then chicken should be immersed in the solution. Keep something heavy on the chicken to keep it immersed in the solution.
3. Cover the bowl and chill for 2 – 4 hours.
4. Crank up the oven to broil mode and set it up to preheat.

Main dish

5. Take out the chicken from the solution and place it in a broiler pan. The remaining solution is to be discarded.
6. Place the pan in the oven, 4 – 5 inches below the heat element and broil for 20 minutes, turning the chicken over half way through broiling.
7. Now set the temperature of the oven to 350° F. Shift the broiling pan to the central rack and bake until the chicken is not pink anymore in the center.
8. Serve immediately.

Coffee-Rubbed Pork Roast

Serves: 3

Ingredients

- 1 ¾ pounds Boston butt or pork shoulder
- ¼ cup brown sugar
- 1 teaspoon salt or to taste
- ½ teaspoon minced garlic
- 1 ½ tablespoons coffee beans, ground in a coffee grinder
- 1 teaspoon cayenne pepper
- Cracked black pepper to taste
- ¼ teaspoon smoked paprika

Directions

1. Mix together ground coffee, brown sugar, salt, garlic, and all the spices in a bowl.
2. Sprinkle the spice mixture on the meat and pat it lightly. Place it in a slow cooker.
3. Close the lid and allow it to cook on low for 6 – 7 hours or until tender.
4. Shred the meat with a pair of forks. Mix it well with the liquid in the slow cooker.
5. Serve hot.

Roasted Portobello Steaks With Walnut Coffee Sauce

❦ *Serves: 2* ❦

Ingredients

Main dish

- 2 extra-large Portobello mushrooms, discard stem
- ½ tablespoon balsamic vinegar
- 1 tablespoon olive oil
- Salt and pepper to taste

For walnut coffee sauce
- 1 ½ tablespoons olive oil
- 2 cloves garlic, chopped
- ⅔ cup black coffee
- ½ teaspoon miso
- 1 extra-large shallot, diced
- ½ cup raw walnuts
- Salt and pepper to taste
- ½ teaspoon balsamic vinegar
- Thyme sprig to garnish

To serve: Use any
- Mashed potatoes
- Cauliflower mash
- Cooked quinoa or wild rice
- Cooked brown rice

Directions

1. Prepare a baking sheet by lining it with parchment paper. Prepare the oven by pre-heating it to 350° F.
2. Combine vinegar and oil in a bowl. Brush this mixture all over the mushrooms. Season with salt and pepper and place it stem side down on the baking sheet.
3. Place the baking sheet in the oven and bake for about 25 minutes or until the mushrooms are tender.
4. Meanwhile, place a saucepan over medium flame. Add oil and let it heat. Once the oil is heated, add garlic and shallot and cook until soft.
5. Stir in the walnuts. Cook for about 2 minutes. Stir frequently.
6. Add coffee and stir. Turn off the heat. Transfer the mixture into a blender. Add salt, miso, pepper, and balsamic vinegar and blend until smooth.
7. Pour the sauce into the pan and heat the sauce.
8. Pour sauce into a bowl. Place mushrooms on top. Slice the mushrooms if desired.
9. Garnish with a thyme sprig and serve with any of the suggested serving options.

Ham With Red-Eye Gravy

∽ *Serves: 8* ∽

Ingredients

- 2 tablespoons vegetable oil
- 8 slices ham, (¼ inch thick slices)
- 1 cup chopped fatty ham scraps
- Salt to taste
- 2 teaspoons all-purpose flour
- Freshly ground pepper to taste
- 1 ⅓ cups brewed coffee
- ¼ teaspoon cayenne pepper or to taste

Main dish

Directions

1. Pour oil into a skillet and heat over medium flame. Add ham scraps and cook until brown.
2. Remove ham scraps with a slotted spoon and place on a plate.
3. Add ham slices into the same skillet and cook until brown on both sides. Sprinkle salt, pepper, and cayenne pepper on each side of the ham.
4. Remove ham with a slotted spoon and place it along with ham scrap.
5. Add flour into the skillet and stir constantly for a couple of minutes. Raise heat to medi-

um-high. Add coffee into the pan, stirring constantly. Keep stirring until thick.

6. Add salt and pepper to taste. Add ham back into the skillet along with ham scrap.
7. Mix well and heat thoroughly.
8. Serve hot.

Salmon Tacos With Coffee Rub

∽ Serves: 2 ∽

Ingredients

- ½ teaspoon chili powder
- ½ teaspoon brown sugar
- ½ teaspoon ground cumin
- Salt to taste
- ¾ teaspoon finely ground coffee
- Freshly ground pepper to taste
- Extra-virgin olive oil, to brush
- 1 tablespoon chopped cilantro
- 2 small cloves garlic, minced
- ½ ripe Hass avocado, peeled, pitted, chopped
- 4 corn tortillas
- 1 salmon fillet (8 ounces) skinless and center-cut
- 1 tomatillo, husked, quartered
- ½ small jalapeño, deseeded, chopped
- 3 tablespoons sour cream
- 1 cup finely shredded red cabbage
- 1 cup finely shredded green cabbage
- Hot sauce to serve
- Lime wedges to serve

Main dish

Directions:

1. Combine cumin, brown sugar, chili powder, salt, pepper, and coffee in a bowl.
2. Brush oil over the salmon fillet. Sprinkle the spice mixture all over the fillet.
3. Place tomatillos, jalapeño, cilantro, and garlic in a blender and blend until smooth.
4. Blend in the sour cream. Finally, place avocado in the blender and give short pulses until smooth.
5. Pour the mixture into a bowl. Add salt and pepper to taste. Add red and green cabbage and stir until cabbage is well coated with the dressing.
6. Brush the tortillas with oil and place them one over the other. Wrap the tortillas in foil and place them in a preheated oven and bake at 300°F for 10 minutes.
7. Place a grill pan over medium flame. Brush oil on the bottom of the grill pan and over the salmon fillet as well.
8. Place salmon fillet in the pan and cook for 4 – 5 minutes. Turn the fillet and cook for 4 – 5 minutes.
9. Remove salmon from the pan and place on a plate. Using a fork, flake the salmon.

10 To assemble: Divide the salmon among the tortillas. Divide the cabbage and place over the salmon.

11 Serve immediately along with hot sauce and lime wedges if desired.

Main dish

Risotto with Capers and Espresso

Serves: 3

Ingredients

- 1 tablespoon salt-packed Pantelleria capers
- 2 ¾ cups chicken stock or low-sodium broth
- ½ small onion, minced
- 2 tablespoons dry white wine
- 2 tablespoons brewed espresso
- 1 tablespoon extra-virgin olive oil
- ¾ cup short grain rice
- 4 espresso beans
- 2 tablespoons freshly grated parmesan cheese
- ½ tablespoon ground espresso powder
- Freshly ground pepper to taste
- 1 tablespoon unsalted butter
- Salt to taste

Directions

1 Place capers in a small bowl. Pour enough water to cover it by about 2 inches. Drain off after an hour. Chop the capers.

2 Pour brewed espresso into a small saucepan and place it over high flame. Let it boil down to 1 tablespoon. Turn off the heat and set it aside.

Main dish

3. Pour stock into a saucepan and let it come to a simmer over low flame. Let it remain on low flame.
4. Pour olive oil into a large saucepan. Place the saucepan over medium-high flame. Once oil is heated, add onions and cook until translucent.
5. Stir in the rice and cook for a couple of minutes, until rice turns slightly opaque.
6. Pour wine and let it cook for about a minute. Add espresso beans and stir.
7. Pour ½ cup of the simmering stock. Lower the heat to medium and keep stirring until dry.
8. Repeat the previous step until all but 1/8 cup of the stock is used up and rice is cooked. By now the risotto should be creamy. Turn off the heat.
9. Pick out the espresso beans and discard it.
10. Add butter and cheese and stir. Stir in 2 tablespoons of the retained stock.
11. Add salt and pepper to taste.
12. To serve: Divide risotto into 3 plates. Garnish with capers and espresso powder. Drizzle 1 teaspoon of the brewed, reduced espresso on each plate and serve.

Chapter 4

Dessert Recipes

Coffee Ice Cream

∞ *Serves: 12 – 14* ∞

Dessert

Ingredients

- 2 ½ cups very chilled heavy or double cream
- 4 tablespoons instant espresso powder
- 1 ⅓ cups sweetened condensed milk
- 4 tablespoons espresso liqueur

Directions

1. Place heavy cream, espresso powder, condensed milk, and espresso liqueur in a bowl. Whisk until soft peaks are formed.
2. Pour into freezer safe containers and freeze until firm.
3. Scoop into bowls and serve.

Chocolate Coffee Toffee Crunch Muffins

∽ Serves: 6 ∽

Ingredients

For muffins
- 1 cup all-purpose flour
- ¼ cup unsweetened cocoa powder, sifted
- ¼ teaspoon baking soda
- 1 teaspoon baking powder
- ¼ teaspoon fine sea salt
- ⅓ cup packed brown sugar
- ½ tablespoon instant espresso powder
- 3 tablespoons unsalted butter, melted
- 1 large egg
- ½ cup semi-sweet chocolate chips
- ¾ cup buttermilk
- ½ teaspoon vanilla extract

For toffee crunch topping
- 2 tablespoons all-purpose flour
- ¼ cup toffee bits
- 1 tablespoon brown sugar
- ½ tablespoon butter, at room temperature

Directions

1. Prepare a 6-count muffin pan by lining it with disposable liners.
2. Combine all the dry ingredients in a bowl — flour, cocoa, baking soda, baking powder, brown sugar, espresso powder, and salt.
3. Whisk together all the wet ingredients in another bowl — buttermilk, butter, vanilla, and eggs.
4. Combine the wet and dry ingredients. Mix until just incorporated, making sure not to overbeat.
5. Add chocolate chips and fold gently.
6. Pour the batter into the muffin cups. Make sure that all the cups have similar quantity of batter.
7. To make toffee crunch topping: Place sugar, flour, and toffee bits in a bowl. Stir until well combined. Add butter and cut it into the mixture using a fork. Stir until small crumbs are formed.
8. Scatter this mixture on top of the batter in the muffin cups.
9. Place the muffin pan in a preheated oven and bake at 375° F for 20 minutes. You can check if the muffins are done by inserting a toothpick in the center of the muffin. Remove the

toothpick. If you see any particles stuck on it, the muffins need to be baked for a few more minutes; if not, remove the muffin pan from the oven and cool on a wire rack for 5 minutes.

10 Take out the muffins from the pan and place on a wire rack to cool.

11 Serve.

Dessert

Double Chocolate Bundt Cake with Ganache Glaze

Serves: 20 – 25

Ingredients

- 10 ounces bittersweet chocolate, chopped, divided
- 2 cups sugar
- 4 cups all-purpose flour
- 2 tablespoons baking soda
- 1 cup Dutch process cocoa powder
- 1 ½ teaspoons salt

- 1 ½ cups canola oil
- 2 large eggs
- 2 cups strong brewed coffee
- ⅔ cup heavy cream
- 1 tablespoon unsalted butter
- 2 cups buttermilk
- 1 tablespoon corn syrup

Directions

1. Grease a large Bundt pan (12 cup size) with cooking spray.
2. Add 4 ounces chocolate into a small saucepan. Place the saucepan over low flame and melt the chocolate, stirring all the while.
3. Transfer the melted chocolate into a bowl. Add oil, egg, and sugar and whisk until well incorporated.
4. Combine coffee and buttermilk in a bowl.
5. Combine all the dry ingredients in a bowl — flour, baking soda, cocoa, and salt.
6. Stir in ¼ of the flour mixture into the bowl. Pour a cup of the buttermilk mixture and stir until well combined and smooth.
7. Repeat the previous steps 3 more times until all the flour mixture and buttermilk mixture is added.

8. Spoon the batter into the Bundt pan.
9. Place rack in the lower third position in the oven and preheat the oven to 350° F.
10. Place the Bundt pan in the oven and bake for 45 minutes.
11. You can check if the cake is done by inserting a toothpick in the center of the cake. Remove the toothpick. If you see any particles stuck on it, the cake needs to be baked for a few more minutes; if not, remove the pan from the oven and cool on a wire rack for 5 minutes. Remove the cake from the pan and place on a plate or cake stand. Let it cool completely.
12. Pour cream into a saucepan and place over low flame. When cream begins to simmer, turn off the heat. Combine remaining chocolate, butter, and corn syrup in a bowl. Pour hot cream over the chocolate mixture and cover for 5 minutes.
13. Stir constantly for a few minutes until smooth. Cool for about 5 – 6 minutes.
14. Pour ganache over the cake and let the cake rest for a while until ganache sets.
15. Slice and serve.

Vietnamese Coffee Sundaes With Crushed Peanut Brittle

∽ *Serves: 8* ∽

Ingredients

- 2 cups + 2 tablespoons sugar
- 2 cups unsalted roasted peanuts
- 2 teaspoons kosher salt
- 4 tablespoons instant coffee mixed with 3 teaspoons hot water
- 4 cups vanilla ice cream
- 1 cup water
- 1 teaspoon ground cinnamon
- 1 ½ cups sweetened condensed milk
- 1 cup heavy cream

Dessert

Directions

1 Grease a baking sheet with some cooking spray. Place 2 cups of sugar in a saucepan. Pour water and stir. Place the saucepan over medium-high flame. When the mixture comes to a boil, do not stir. Soon the color of the solution will change from white to caramel. Turn off the heat.

2. Add peanuts, salt, and cinnamon and stir until peanuts are well coated with the mixture.
3. Spread the mixture on the baking sheet. Let it rest until hard.
4. Chop 8 pieces from the peanut brittle. Place the rest of the brittle in a Ziploc bag. Seal the bag and crush into smaller pieces by banging slightly with a rolling pin until smaller in size.
5. Combine condensed milk and coffee in a bowl. Whisk until well combined.
6. Place cream and 2 tablespoons sugar in a mixing bowl. Beat with an electric hand mixer until soft peaks are formed.
7. Take 8 dessert glasses. Place ½ cup ice cream in each glass. Drizzle condensed milk mixture in the glasses.
8. Scatter the smaller pieces of peanut brittle in each glass. Divide the whipped cream among the glasses.
9. Insert one of the bigger brittle pieces in each glass and serve right away.

Chocolate Pudding

∞ Serves: 10 – 12 ∞

Ingredients

- 10 ounces bittersweet chocolate, chopped
- 4 2/3 cups whole milk
- 1/4 teaspoon salt
- 2 tablespoons cornstarch
- 4 teaspoons pure vanilla extract
- Mildly sweetened whipped cream to serve
- 4 tablespoons unsalted butter
- 1 cup sugar
- 4 tablespoons Dutch process cocoa
- 4 large egg yolks
- 2 large whole eggs
- 3 teaspoons instant espresso

Dessert

Directions

1. Have an ice bath ready. Place a bowl with a strainer on top of it over the ice bath.
2. Place chocolate and butter in a microwave safe bowl. Cook on high for about a minute or until chocolate melts. Whisk until smooth and let it cool.

3. Pour 4 cups milk into a saucepan. Add ½ cup sugar and salt and place the saucepan over medium flame. Stir frequently until sugar dissolves completely.
4. Combine cornstarch, 2/3 cup milk, and cocoa powder in another bowl. Pour the cocoa mixture into the saucepan and whisk well.
5. Whisk together egg yolks, whole eggs, and ½ cup sugar in a bowl. Pour some of the warmed milk and whisk well.
6. Pour this mixture into the saucepan and raise the heat to medium. Whisk constantly until it is very thick. Turn off the heat.
7. Add the melted chocolate mixture, espresso, and vanilla and whisk until well combined.
8. Pour the pudding into the prepared bowl on the ice bath. Strain the mixture into the bowl.
9. Discard the solids. Keep stirring the pudding until it cools down.
10. Cover the pudding with cling wrap (the cling wrap should touch the pudding) so that film does not form on top of the pudding.
11. Chill for 4 – 8 hours.
12. Top with whipped cream and serve.

Bittersweet Chocolate Tart With Coffee Mascarpone Cream

∽ Serves: 18 – 20 ∽

Ingredients

For tart shells
- 2 ⅔ cups all-purpose flour
- ⅛ teaspoon salt
- 2 large egg yolks
- 1 ½ cups confectioner's sugar
- 14 tablespoons unsalted butter, softened

For chocolate custard
- 1 ½ cups heavy cream
- 1 pound bitter-sweet chocolate, chopped
- 1 cup whole milk
- 2 large eggs, beaten

For toppings
- 2 ½ teaspoons unflavored gelatin
- 3 teaspoons pure coffee extract or 3 teaspoons espresso powder mixed with 3 teaspoons water
- 2 ¾ cups mascarpone cheese
- 2 tablespoons unsweetened cocoa powder
- 4 tablespoons cold water
- 3 cups heavy cream
- ½ cup sugar

Dessert

Directions

1. Place flour, salt, and confectioners' sugar in the food processor bowl. Process until well combined.
2. Mix in the egg yolks and butter. You should get tiny crumbs of the mixture.
3. Take 2 tart pans (9 – 10 inches each) that have bottoms that are removable.
4. Divide the dough among the pans. Press it onto the bottom as well as the sides of the pan.
5. Chill for about an hour or until hard.
6. Place a sheet of parchment paper on the crust as well. Place pie weights or a packet of dried beans on the pie crusts and place the pie pans in an oven that has been preheated to 350° F and bake for 30 minutes.
7. Take off the pie weights and parchment paper. Keep the edges of the pie pan covered with foil and continue baking until golden brown.
8. Remove pie pans from the oven and let cool on a wire rack.
9. To make chocolate custard: Combine milk and cream in a saucepan. Place the saucepan over medium flame and stir often until bubbly. Turn off the heat.

10. Stir in the chocolate and let it rest for a couple of minutes. Stir vigorously until smooth. Let it rest for 10 minutes.
11. Add eggs and whisk well. The mixture would have thickened a bit.
12. Remove the tart shells from the pie pans and place it on a large baking sheet.
13. Pour chocolate custard over the tart shells.
14. Pop the baking sheet into the oven and bake until the edges are set and it will be jelly-like in the middle.
15. Cool completely on a wire rack. Chill for 6 – 8 hours.
16. To make topping: Pour water into a saucepan. Scatter gelatin on top and let it rest for 5 minutes.
17. Stir in coffee extract. Place the saucepan over low flame. Once gelatin melts, turn off the heat and let it cool for a few minutes.
18. Place mascarpone cheese, cream, and sugar in a mixing bowl. Beat with an electric hand mixer until firm peaks are formed.
19. With the mixer running on low speed, add the gelatin mixture into the bowl. Beat until well incorporated.
20. Decorate the tarts with the whipped cream. Dust the cocoa over the whipped cream.
21. Chill until the topping sets.

Mini Tiramisu

Serves: 8

Ingredients

- 1 cup whole milk
- 8 egg yolks
- 4 containers (8 ounces each) mascarpone cheese
- ½ cup rum or brandy (optional)
- Cocoa powder, as required
- 1 ⅓ cups sugar, divided
- 2 teaspoons pure vanilla extract
- 2 cups brewed coffee, cooled to room temperature
- 48 ladyfingers cookies

Directions

1. Combine milk and 2/3 cup sugar in a pot and place the pot over medium-low flame. Stir often until sugar dissolves completely.
2. Meanwhile, place egg yolks in a bowl along with vanilla extract and 2/3 cup sugar. Whisk until well combined.
3. When the milk begins to bubble around the edges, drizzle the milk mixture into the bowl of yolks, stirring constantly while adding.
4. Pour the mixture back into the pot and cook over low flame until the mixture is thick, stirring constantly. It should coat the back part of the spoon.
5. Pour the mixture into a bowl. Cover the custard with cling wrap. It should touch the custard. This is done to prevent the formation of film on top of the custard.
6. Chill for 40 – 50 minutes or until it comes to room temperature.
7. Add mascarpone cheese and whisk until well incorporated.
8. Combine alcohol and coffee in a bowl. Have ready 8 dessert glasses on your countertop.
9. Immerse a ladyfinger for about 12 – 15 seconds in the coffee mixture and place it on the bottom of a glass. If the ladyfinger is not fitting

well into the glass, break it into 2 pieces. Do this once again, so you have 2 ladyfinger cookies in each glass.

10. Repeat the previous step and place the cookies in the remaining glasses.
11. Pour ¼ cup of the custard over the cookies, in each of the glasses.
12. Repeat the layering of cookies and custard (step 9 – 11) in the glasses. In all you should have 3 layers of each – cookies and custard in each glass, with custard being the topmost layer.
13. Chill for 45 – 60 minutes.
14. Garnish with cocoa powder on top and serve.

Chapter 5

Drink Recipes

Choco Fudge Protein Shake

∽ Serves: 2 ∽

Ingredients

- 2 cups milk of your choice
- 2 tablespoons chocolate protein powder
- ⅛ teaspoon salt
- 2 – 4 tablespoons peanut butter or almond butter
- 3 teaspoons cocoa powder
- 2 teaspoons instant coffee powder
- ½ teaspoon pure vanilla extract
- 2 very ripe bananas, sliced, frozen
- Sweetener of your choice (optional)

Directions

1. Place milk, chocolate protein powder, salt, peanut butter, cocoa powder, coffee powder, vanilla extract, bananas, and sweetener in a blender.
2. Blitz until smooth.
3. Pour into 2 glasses and serve.

The Layaway

Serves: 2

Ingredients

- 4 ounces spiced rum
- 1 ounce fresh lemon juice
- 4 ounces strong black coffee, at room temperature
- 8 ounces ginger beer, chilled

Directions

1. Pour rum, lemon juice, and coffee into a cocktail shaker. Add ice cubes to fill up the shaker.
2. Close the shaker and shake constantly for about 20 seconds.
3. Pour into 2 glasses. Pour 4 ounces ginger beer in each glass and serve.

Siciliano

Serves: 2

Ingredients

- 3 ounces strong brewed coffee, chilled
- 4 ounces sweet vermouth (Italian if possible)
- Club soda, as required
- 2 ounces simple syrup
- 3 ounces amaro
- 2 round, thin slices orange, to garnish

Directions

1. Pour vermouth, coffee, amaro, and simple syrup into a cocktail shaker. Add ice cubes to fill up the shaker.
2. Close the shaker and shake constantly for about 20 seconds.
3. Pour into 2 glasses. Pour club soda into the glasses.
4. Make a small slit in each orange slice.
5. Insert the orange on the rim of the glass and serve.

Iced Coffee Shakerato

≈ Serves: 2 ≈

Ingredients

- 3 ounces espresso coffee or 6 ounces very strong coffee, slightly cooled
- 3 teaspoons simple syrup
- 2 tablespoons sweetened condensed milk

Directions

1. Pour espresso, simple syrup, and condensed milk into a cocktail shaker. Add ice cubes to fill up the shaker.
2. Close the shaker and shake constantly for about 30 seconds.
3. Place some crushed ice in 2 glasses. Strain and pour the drink into the glasses.
4. Serve.

Iced Horchata Latte

Serves: 2

Ingredients

- ⅛ cup brown rice
- ⅛ cup raw almonds
- ⅛ cup sugar
- 1 tablespoon coffee beans
- 1 inch stick cinnamon, crushed
- A pinch salt
- 2 cups + ⅛ cup water

Directions

1. Grind the rice in a spice grinder or coffee grinder until coarse in texture.
2. Place ground rice, cinnamon, almonds and 2 cups water in an airtight container.
3. Grind the coffee beans in the spice grinder or coffee grinder until coarse in texture.
4. Add it into the airtight container (with the ground rice mixture) and stir well.
5. Close the lid and chill for 7 – 8 hours.
6. Pour 1/8 cup water into a small saucepan. Add sugar and stir. Place the saucepan over

medium flame and stir until sugar dissolves completely.

7. Pour into a bowl. Cover and place the bowl in the refrigerator for 30 minutes.
8. Blend the contents of the airtight container in a blender until really smooth.
9. Place a fine wire mesh strainer over a bowl and strain the mixture into the bowl. Press to remove most of the liquid.
10. Add the sugar syrup and salt and stir until well combined.
11. Place crushed ice in 2 glasses. Pour the latte into the glasses and serve.

Drink

Mochatini (Mocha Martini)

Serves: 2

Ingredients

- 1 ½ ounces chocolate liqueur
- 3 ounces coffee liqueur + extra for rimming
- 3 ounces vanilla vodka
- Sugar, for rimming
- Finely grated white chocolate, for rimming

Directions

1. Take 2 glasses and moisten the rims of the glasses with coffee liqueur.
2. Combine white chocolate and sugar on a plate. Dredge the rims of the glasses in this mixture.
3. Pour coffee liqueur, chocolate liqueur, and vanilla vodka into a cocktail shaker. Add ice cubes to fill up the shaker.
4. Close the shaker and shake constantly for about 15 – 20 seconds.
5. Pour into the prepared glasses and serve.

Caramel Irish Coffee

Serves: 2

Ingredients

- 2 ounces Irish whiskey
- 2 ounces butterscotch schnapps
- 2 ounces Irish cream
- 5 ounces freshly brewed hot coffee or use more if required
- Caramel syrup, to garnish
- Whipped cream to garnish

Directions

1. Take 2 Irish coffee glasses or mugs and fill it up with hot water. Let the water remain in the glasses for 5 – 6 minutes.
2. Combine Irish whiskey, butterscotch schnapps, Irish cream and coffee in a pitcher. Stir until well combined.
3. Discard the water from the glasses.
4. Pour coffee mixture into the glasses.
5. Pipe some whipped cream on top. Top with caramel syrup and serve.

Coffee Smoothie

Serves: 4

Ingredients

- 2 cups strong brewed coffee, cooled to room temperature
- ½ cup rolled oats
- 2 tablespoons flaxseed meal
- 2 cups soy milk
- 2 bananas, sliced
- 2 tablespoons cocoa powder
- ¼ teaspoon ground cinnamon
- 2 teaspoons honey

Directions

1. Freeze brewed coffee in ice cube trays until firm.
2. Place coffee ice cubes, rolled oats, flaxseed meal, soymilk, bananas, cocoa powder, honey, and cinnamon in a blender and blitz until smooth.
3. Pour into 2 glasses and serve.

Mint Mojito Iced Coffee

∽ Serves: 2 ∽

Ingredients

- 2 cups freshly brewed, strong coffee
- 2 tablespoons sweetener of your choice
- Cream or half and half or milk of your choice to serve (optional)
- 24 large fresh mint leaves + extra mint sprigs to garnish
- 2 cups ice

Directions

1. Place sweetener and mint in a cocktail shaker. Muddle the mixture with the back of a wooden spoon or muddler.
2. Add ice as required. Add hot coffee into the shaker. Close the lid and shake constantly until chilled.
3. Pour into 2 glasses. Add some crushed ice if desired.
4. Drizzle a little cream if using. Place a mint sprig in each glass and serve.

Salted Caramel Mocha Coffee Concentrate

∽ Serves: 10 ∽

Ingredients

- 8 cups cold brewed coffee or ½ cup instant coffee mixed with 8 cups hot water
- 4 tablespoons cocoa powder
- ½ teaspoon butter extract (optional)
- 10 medjool dates, pitted, soaked in a bowl of hot water for about 5 minutes
- 2 teaspoons vanilla extract
- ½ teaspoon sea salt

Directions

1. If you prefer instant coffee, you need not soak the dates in hot water. You can soak it in the instant coffee itself.
2. Place dates in a blender. Add a little of the coffee and blend until smooth.
3. Add remaining coffee, cocoa powder, butter extract, vanilla extract, dates, and sea salt and blend until smooth. You can blend in batches if required.

4. Strain if desired. If you wish to strain, pour the mixture into a nut milk bag and strain the mixture.
5. Pour into a jar and chill until use.
6. To use: Fill glasses with ice. Add the concentrate as per your taste. Pour milk of your choice and stir.
7. Serve.

Chapter 6

Uses of Coffee in Your Home

Apart from the obvious use of consumption, coffee can also be used for other functions in your home. Here are a few:

To Remove Odor From Your Refrigerator

If there is meat stench or any general stale smell in your refrigerator then place used, leftover coffee grounds in a bowl. Place the bowl at the back of the refrigerator and let it remain overnight. Discard the coffee grounds in the morning. Even if your refrigerator does not smell, it is a good practice to keep a small bowl of coffee grounds in the refrigerator to keep your refrigerator smelling fresh. Discard the coffee after 15 days and replace with fresh coffee.

To Remove Odor From Hands

To remove the smell of onions, garlic, fish and any other strong odor from your hands, moisten your hands with a little water and rub coffee grounds for about 20-30 seconds. Wash your hands with lukewarm water, or a mild soap if needed.

As a Fertilizer

Coffee beans work as excellent fertilizer. Crush some egg shells and mix it with coffee grounds and use it as a fertilizer for vegetables and fruits like tomatoes, cucumbers, carrots, radishes, blueberries and strawberries. Do not use it on all the vegetables as coffee grounds are very acidic. Mixing coffee grounds with orange peels and placing it in your garden if it is infested with pests, such as ants, snails, etc., will help keep the pests at bay. You can also spray brewed coffee directly on the pests.

To Clean Dishes

Coffee grounds help remove grease and stubborn food particles that are stuck to your dishes. For this, place 2 to 3 teaspoons of coffee grounds in a bowl. Add enough warm water to make a thick solution. Dip a sponge in this solution and clean your dishes just like you would use normal dish soap. You can also use this to clean the stovetop.

To Clean Grill and Stains on Kitchen Tiles

Brew some coffee and pour it into a washing tub. Place the grill grates in the tub for 45 minutes. Scrub the grill and wash it off with warm water. Take some warm soap water and add some coffee grounds to it. Dip a dishcloth in this solution and rub the stains with it. Wipe off with plain water.

To Clean and Repair Scratches on Wooden Furniture

Combine a tablespoon of coffee and a little warm water in a bowl. Rub the scratches on your furniture with it.

To Clean Drains

If you have clogged drains, place some coffee grounds in the clogged drain. Pour some liquid soap over the coffee grounds. Finally pour boiling water on top.

To Repel Fleas From Pets

Sprinkle coffee grounds on your dogs or cats fur coat and spread it all over. This should drive out the fleas. In case you are using some medications on your pet, mix coffee grounds and the medication and apply on the fur coat.

To Clean Countertops

If there are stubborn, leftover food particles stuck on your countertop, dab a cloth with used coffee grounds and rub the stained area with it.

Conclusion

I want to thank you once again for choosing this book. I hope you enjoyed these coffee recipes!

After going through all the different recipes given in this book, you should have realized that coffee can be added to every single meal of your day. Also, coffee recipes don't necessarily have to be sweet beverages. The naturally bitter, bold, and earthy flavors and aromas of coffee beans pair incredibly well with red meats and pork. While cooking with coffee, ensure that you always use a fresh brew of strong coffee, unless the recipe specifically calls for coffee grounds. Unless the recipe instructions explicitly specify using hot coffee, ensure that the brew is at room temperature before you add it to any dish.

Cooking with coffee will introduce you to a whole new array of bold and wonderful flavors and ingredient pairings. If you cannot get enough caffeine, think about incorporating this wonderful ingredient into your cooking. If you have a little extra brewed coffee or even coffee grounds lying around, you can pretty much perk up any dish with it. The only thing you need to do is understand the different flavor combinations that work well with coffee. Whether you want to add freshly brewed coffee to alcoholic beverages such as a mocha martini or infuse it into dessert recipes, there is a lot you can do. The good news is you don't have to spend hours on the Internet looking for cooking ideas and recipes using coffee. All the recipes you need are given in this book.

This book is filled with delicious recipes and ideas well-suited for all coffee lovers. From incorporating coffee into marinades and spice rubs to making desserts and drinks infused with coffee, the options are unlimited. All it takes is a desire to experiment with various flavor combinations and pairings. What more? All the recipes given in this book can be easily customized and adjusted according to your palate. These recipes are incredibly easy to understand and simple to follow. You don't need any fancy or expensive ingredients to cook delicious food. Also, you don't have to spend hours in the kitchen cooking with these ingredients. Simple food infused with the bold and earthy aroma of coffee will truly elevate your cooking game within no time!

Whenever you think about adding coffee to desserts or even drinks, you have the option of choosing between regular and flavored coffees. So, which one can you choose? The answer is entirely up to you. As a rule of thumb, it is always better to stick with unflavored coffee for savory dishes. With dessert recipes, you can experiment a little. Flavored coffee grounds can help enhance the overall flavor profile of desserts. So, experiment a little!

Now, all that's left for you to do is gather the required ingredients, keep your favorite brew on hand, and select a recipe that strikes your fancy. After this, you merely need to follow the simple instructions, and voila! Cooking with coffee will open up an entirely new dimension of dishes that will tingle your taste buds. Once you get the hang of the various flavor combinations, let your imagination guide the way. So, what are you waiting for? There is no time like the present to get started! Thank you and all the best!

Suggested Readings

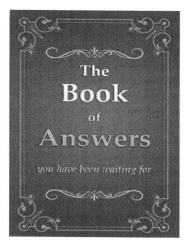

"Cuore d'oro libri" is a new reality that aims at publishing books that have at their core the joyous and serene evolution of the heart, mind and soul. Please visit our website and subscribe to our newsletter to be informed about our news and walk with us in this exatraordinary adventure called life.
Thank you for reading this book.
Let's spread gratitude together and the world will smile.

www.heartofgoldbooks.com

www.ivannossa.com

References

Check out our favorite tips and recipes for cooking and baking with coffee. (2020, February 11). Coffee with the Queen. https://thequeenbean.blog/2020/02/11/check-out-our-favorite-tips-and-recipes-for-cooking-and-baking-with-coffee/

Hutson, C. (2017, September 10). *A definitive guide to the 4 main types of coffee beans | Atlas Coffee Club*. Atlas Coffee Club Blog | Club Culture. https://club.atlascoffeeclub.com/4-main-types-of-coffee-beans/

Oxenreider, T. (2013). *Coffee: a brief history, how it gets to your cup (and what do those labels mean?)*. The Art of Simple. https://theartofsimple.net/coffee/#:~:text=Coffee%20was%20birthed%20in%20the

Printed in Great Britain
by Amazon